YOGA STORIES FOR HEALTHY LIVING

MINA SEMYON

BALBOA.
PRESS

A DIVISION OF HAY HOUSE

Balboa Press books may be ordered through booksellers or by contacting:

Balboa Press
A Division of Hay House
1663 Liberty Drive
Bloomington, IN 47403
www.balboapress.com
1 (877) 407-4847

Print information available on the last page.

ISBN: 978-1-5043-3324-5 (sc)
ISBN: 978-1-5043-3325-2 (e)

Balboa Press rev. date: 09/02/2015

Dedication

I dedicate this book to Arthur Balaskas who was the first shore I ever reached

With Gratitude

To Ronnie Laing, my teacher and friend, who started me off on the voyage out of my wretched mind towards open heartedness and love

To Mary Ann Ephgrave for her love, encouragement and major contribution in bringing this book to life

To Xanthe Berkeley for the flowing photo session and beautiful photographs

To my lovely family, Kira, Alexi, Guillermo and Snow Tiger the Cat and my extended family Janet, Kim, Ias, Joanna, Theo, Nina, Agung, Narayan, Dominic, Ilias, Satya for all the fun, love and support

To all my students who continuously inspire me to deepen my connection to the Source

To old friends and new friends for kindness, laughter and peace of mind.

To all the staff at Balboa Press for doing what they said they would do

Take care of yourself -- you never know when the world will need you.

- Rabbi Hillel

Distracted in a Ditch

'The centipede was happy quite
Until a toad in fun
Said, 'Pray, which leg comes after which?'
This raised her mind to such a pitch,
She lay distracted in the ditch, considering how to run'

I called my first book 'The Distracted Centipede' because of the ditty's essential message: *we lose our wholeness when our head gets in the way.* Before the centipede got her head done in by the toad she didn't need to 'know' how to run.

When we are discombobulated, fragmented, moving too fast, worried about what other people think, we are like the Distracted Centipede; we lose touch with our inner knowing and go to experts to find out how we should walk, what we should eat, how much we should drink, what is too much? We need a psychiatrist to tell us that what we experience has a label called 'depression'. We've lost our connection to the place inside that 'knows'.

So we need to slow down; stop, breathe, feel and get to know that inner being that is in touch with all the wisdom we need, our childlike nature, curious, trusting, playful and knowing.

I'm just in love with the state of wholeness of the centipede before the toad did her head in. So the Distracted Centipede's journey continues in my second book, going deeper into retrieving the wholeness; becoming centered and grounded. Yoga with Mindfulness and Breathing is a path towards that wholeness.

We mustn't underestimate what a deep journey it is to really become aware of the breath - coming and going - from that amazing magical Source that breathes us and keeps us alive, the same source that walks the centipede.

What every centipede knows

The body doesn't need our interference;
it is a unified system to which we can safely surrender
if we let go of holding on for dear life

The centipede is 'programmed' to be a centipede; it simply can't deviate or go astray. It doesn't need workshops on how to deal with the complexity of all its legs, provided that it doesn't get distracted 'by a toad'. Human beings do get distracted therefore more can go wrong with the human being than the centipede. By becoming distracted we become fragmented and lose the sense of our unified being.

To live in the place of deep connectedness requires being present and aware at every moment. Of all living creatures only human beings resist and deny the need for being present and aware.

If you stop at any moment and ask yourself 'where am I?' Like this story about the Rabbi who comes into his congregation and says 'Shalom'. A few minutes later he says 'Shalom' again, and then a few minutes later 'Shalom' again, till one of the members asks, 'why do you keep on saying shalom?' The Rabbi replies, 'Because you weren't here.'

A Woman of a Certain Age

All the herbs and diets in the world won't help if we don't know how to slow down and 'go with the flow'. Ignorance is going against the flow and not even knowing that there is a flow. We dig our heels in, resist life as it is and wonder why we are feeling out of it. And then blame it on the Bossa Nova!

If we become conscious of our feet on the ground and our spine releasing from the root upwards, let our head balance and allow our breath to flow, we'll experience wholeness and youthfulness, at least for a moment. Let such moments accumulate!

And sometimes I personally 'lose it'. Who doesn't? But I don't feel that because I still lose the plot from time to time it devalues my insights or makes me into a fraud. If habitual patterns still come up I hope to be able to recognize them. The practice I am talking about helps to develop skills to notice and to deal with what comes up, helps to make us less frightened to let it come up, to 'lose it'. If we are not frightened of 'losing it' we don't have to hold onto it and we might eventually realise that there was nothing to hold onto and no need to hold on in the first place!

The other day I was shopping at 'Fresh and Wild' organic food shop. As I was paying, the assistant said, 'Do you know that as a mature citizen you are entitled to 5% discount?'

To be honest at that moment I would much rather have paid the full price than be recognized as a mature citizen!

'I am tired,' I caught myself thinking, 'I don't look my best.'

Akh! All this trying to hang on to the illusion of being young and still attractive to the opposite sex for one more day, and missing out on being who I am at this moment and the wisdom that comes with it.

Cultivating awareness of life opens the way to a more balanced, rhythmical, supple way of being, no matter what age.

When someone says to you, 'You look so young today,' is it really a compliment?

When a young actress said to Mae West at her seventieth birthday party, 'Darling you don't look seventy,' Mae West replied, 'This is what seventy looks like!'

It's really weird, the stigma attached to being a 'woman of a certain age'. Suddenly you feel you are being labelled, isolated, put into a category, put in a box. It's not unlike racism. You are being treated in a certain way, which has nothing to do with who you are. So yes, it helps to practice mindfulness and Yoga with breathing, so you don't get caught up in the image others project on you out of their own needs and limitations. To me Yoga has given me the confidence to not let other people's limitations define me. It's a good thing that preoccupation with age is genuinely receding into irrelevance, giving way to joy of celebrating life and sharing it with others.

Often what we call 'health' is really just a habit we got used to!

Slow down, become still, and listen within. How do you feel?

I ask L: 'How are you?'

'Fine,' she says, with a bright smile on her face. We do some breathing and relaxing. After a while she says, 'I didn't realise how heavy my head feels and I have pain in my shoulders.'

'So how are you really?' I ask.

'Oh, I have a new job. I need an office and they say there isn't a spare room available and it's all just too much. That's why I'm feeling like this – I'm just stressed out. How do I feel? That's a very good question.'

It seems to me that 'stressed out' has become a way of evading how we really feel. 'Stressed out' is not a feeling. It's a way of avoiding feelings. When we start paying attention and learn to connect with our thoughts and feelings in an 'embodied' way and take responsibility for them, we stop blaming them on circumstances or other people. Feelings that aren't connected to the breath become concretised and dumped into the body. Much of our illness is blockage of energy.

'It runs in the family'

We say, 'It runs in the family!' But it only runs in the family because we let it. We need to get 'the grannies out of our groins' - the centuries of inhibitions and prohibitions that sit there, stopping us from claiming freedom and spontaneity.

What Jung calls "participation mystique," is the deep enmeshment that can happen in intimate relationships when an individual doesn't do the inner-work to heal their unconscious pain. The wounds get passed through the generations, metastasizing through our relationships and literally shaping our children's lives. The sickness will stay in the family tree until someone in the outer branches has enough support and awareness to face and move through that ancient grief.

Robustness

'If you take umbrage at every rub how will you become a polished mirror?'

Rumi

In Yiddish umbrage, a sense of slight or injury is called 'farible'. In my childhood everyone was always keeping a 'farible'. No wonder everyone was always complaining of ailments, 'akh, akh my back, oy, oy, my knees'. How can your body relax if it's full of 'faribles'?

When we acknowledge and let go of our resentments and forgive, we come into the spaciousness of the present moment and become tougher and not so precious and touchy about our fragile egos that can't take a drop of truth without falling apart or becoming aggressively defensive.

Conscious Eating

If you close your mouth to food
you can know a sweeter taste

Rumi

My mother's greatest pleasures in life were to watch me eat or to fantasize about me marrying a millionaire. Since millionaires were even harder to come by than food in post-war Russia, as soon as rationing was over my mother really made me eat! So overeating became a device for cutting off painful feelings. When, for the first time in my life, I went on a fast of lemon and honey drinks for a week, I became free of the tyranny of my usual preoccupations and worries. I thought, 'This is it! This is enlightenment!' I felt calm and contented, filled with benign sensations in my body. After a few fasts I began to notice that in between feeling inspired and light, or dejected and lifeless, there was a loaf of bread with butter and jam!

But eating as a means of relieving anxiety and insecurity destroys energy.

The stomach becomes overburdened and we become sleepy and lazy, there is an illusion of relief from anxiety, in fact it is a dulling. The consequences are that we cannot achieve what we have set out to achieve. Gluttony leads away from communication to solitary gratification, which does not satisfy. I noticed there was a connection between believing in my dreams and losing that belief according to how much I ate. The ancient Hawaiian shamans believed that the seat of the low self was in the intestinal tract and the low self was the place where convictions of unworthiness and guilt had to be sought and removed. Maybe that was one of the reasons why my mother kept urging 'eat, eat, my child'. Guilt had to be fed and kept alive at all costs!

It is a deep-seated problem, this overeating, and a very common one, and yet there isn't a quick solution. To change this monster habit on a deep level is to discover its root by doing the inner work and realizing how deeply our relationship with food affects the balance of the body and mind. Getting in touch with the sense of balance and becoming more attuned to it makes us more reluctant to lose it through overeating or eating unconsciously.

How can we change our eating habits?

Practicing Yoga with mindfulness helps to awaken and trust our intuition so that we know when to eat, what to eat and how much to eat. If we are in touch with ourselves we don't need to be told by experts.

Yogis advise not to eat until the breath flows freely through the right and the left nostril. In the physical and subtle bodies there are a certain number of nadis (subtle channels through which energy flows) and chakras (centres in which cosmic energy exists).

The nadis emphasized in Yoga are ida, pingala and susumna. Ida and Pingala represent the sun and the moon, the right is the sun, the left the moon, the male and female principles. Susumna is the central channel in the spinal column and is regarded in Yoga as the road to nirvana, which means cessation of all the spinning in the mind. To breathe freely through the right and left nostrils is to unify the two breaths, and free the central channel.

Alternate nostril breathing is a simple and important exercise for our digestion and general health to practice every morning before eating

Don't hold your breath

Breathe in – breathe out! Look around you.

Without labeling anything, see this moment fresh and new

If someone next to you is holding their breath notice how it affects your breathing. You'll find yourself holding your breath, too, unless you become conscious of it and able to let go. We tend to overlook how we affect each other on such basic levels. So the more harmonious and in touch we are with our breathing the more harmonious our being and being with each other. 'Conspire' literally means 'to breathe together.'

Where Is It Supposed to Hurt?

The Buddha said, *'Our sorrows and wounds are healed only when we touch them with compassion'*

A Yoga student asks, pointing to her left hip: 'Is this where it's supposed to hurt?'

'It hurts where it hurts. Feel where it hurts and breathe into it. You can release tension by breathing and attending to your unique experience of the posture and notice how the pain begins to dissolve. Then you won't need to ask where it is supposed to hurt.'

Pain is a way of drawing your attention to blocked energy. It's not that 'pain is good for you' but often we only start paying attention when it hurts.

All concepts of how it 'ought to be' have to be dropped in order to experience the body directly. It's your body!

Like someone who had a dream that she was being chased by a gorilla. She ran with all her might and suddenly came to a precipice with the gorilla right behind her. She stopped, looked back and asked the gorilla: 'What shall I do?' The gorilla replied: 'I don't know. It's your dream.'

Using what comes up to grow towards being in the present

F: I've found the experience of Yoga with you so different from all the other teachers I have had. You talk about using whatever comes up to grow towards being able to live in the present, by going through it and getting to know it, rather than avoiding and repressing it. To me that's the difference – you allow that we've got what we've got, dark, ugly as it may seem, sometimes that's all we've got to work with.

Mina: Yes, it's true; it's vital to connect bodily posture with thoughts, emotions and breathing.

F: I don't believe that people tie up enough the connection between the psyche and the body. But you talk about it all the time in class, that psychological blocks are locked and stored in the body and by becoming aware of and releasing the tensions we can become aware of what's hiding there and eventually free ourselves by letting go. For instance, when you told me that you had been living in your neck all your pre-Yoga life, it made me aware that so had I. At first I found it hard to make that connection, but now I can feel where these blocks are. And that they are not only physical. All that history stuck in my neck makes it impossible to have clarity about what's really going on in the present moment.

The moment you slow down and say hello to the present moment,
meaning and vitality are here to greet you.

Oh To Be At Ease!

What does it mean – to relax; to be 'relaxed'?

ease: in Latin, means elbows akimbo, having elbowroom.

To relax consciously we need first to become aware of and acknowledge that we are not relaxed. Ease comes from being grounded, with the mind, body and breath balanced and in tune. Anxiety is the result of cutting off feelings in the present moment. Suppressed feelings and emotions create tension that can lead to mental imbalance and physical dis-ease; most of the time we don't realize that we are suppressing our feelings. But if we get into the habit of paying attention to them, acknowledging and releasing them, and at the same time connecting to our breathing, we could heal ourselves before a physical or emotional crisis develops. For me the only time I can say I am truly relaxed and not a danger to myself or others is when I am in a state of acceptance, even acceptance of my non acceptance.

"... and all this you learnt from Yoga

T. sits on the floor with his legs stretched out in front in the Yoga posture Parshchimotanasana. I say, 'Follow your breath and allow the muscles in your legs to relax, so that they can release to the floor. Feel how the tension in your legs is pulling them up to the ceiling. Breathe and let gravity relax them down.'

T. tries to push his legs down with his hands, tightening his shoulders in the process. 'I need two sandbags to hold my legs down.' he says.

'Sandbags are a temporary solution. Breathing and releasing consciously is the more lasting one. It will get you in touch with what makes you hold on. Feel your legs making contact with the ground, let the contact get deeper.'

'No, I need two sandbags.'

I go and lie across his legs like a big sandbag, breathing and enjoying myself.

He relaxes for a moment. After a while I get up.

T says to his friend, 'It's great to have a woman lie on top of your legs like this and not feel any pressure to have to do anything.'

'In intimate situations the pressure to do something is often an obstacle to allowing the spontaneous closeness to happen. If only lovers could breathe deeply and freely they would move naturally to sexual intimacy. It would open before us a thousand and one nights of wonders and delights beyond our wildest dreams. Fidelity would become a natural condition, if only both partners would engage in the process of seeing each other and themselves with fresh eyes, which is the meaning of respect. It is worth reminding ourselves that in lovemaking we may open to the earliest feelings of intimacy and the earliest hurt. Can I trust you with my heart? Can you trust me with your heart? It is a constant process of letting go of what stands in the way of being open and loving. If both partners are open to explore this journey then there is hope for true intimacy, for God's sake.

Sex life would have that quality of the unexpected and new without trying to contrive it with sexy underwear, not that I'm against sexy underwear. Eros resides in tenderness. We don't need pornographic magazines or videos to turn us on, if we relax and let it happen. One relationship could remain an adventure for a lifetime... I think.'

'And all this you learnt from Yoga?'

'Yes'.

Meeting the Buddha at Tesco's

Woke up this morning with worries on my mind! Did all my morning rituals and practices: glass of hot water and lemon, shower, Yoga, Chi Gung, alkaline juice, prayers, and went for a walk on Primrose Hill. While walking I was saying the Ho'oponopono mantra, then stood next to my favorite tree and did some more Chi Gung exercises. The sun was just rising, the air felt fresh. Walking back felt my intensity levels have gone down from 10 to around 5. Stopped at Tesco's to buy some organic blueberries and raspberries for breakfast! Walk into the shop and see only raspberries. A tall beautiful black guy is wiping the floor. I say to him: 'No blueberries? He says, 'Relax.' I didn't quite believe what I heard, so I asked: 'What did you say?' He says as calmly as the first time: 'Relax.' That hit the spot, my intensity levels went down to zero, I started laughing, said: 'Thank you' and laughed all the way home.

Yoga helped me survive Stalin and a Jewish mother

I was introduced to Yoga in therapy by R.D. Laing, who said, 'To talk about your traumatic life is not enough even to a nice chap like me.'

Through the practice of yoga and mindfulness I gained a sense of what is truly essential. I never had an inclination to speculate on whether I was born before and whether I will be born again or whether or not there is such a thing as reincarnation. All I notice is that how I think, speak and behave affects my life here and now and how I 'incarnate' into the next moment. And there *is* something I can do about it. I became less concerned about what other people think of me, they'll think of something else in a minute. Being *authentic* became more important than being *good*.

I feel that being *authentic* has to be good for our individual and collective well being. I somehow don't think that in primitive tribes teenagers need to rebel, because what they learn from adults is sensible training for living life. What our teenagers see is often so twisted and disconnected that when they start thinking for themselves they want to get away from it as far as possible. I once saw a picture of a girl with rings pierced through her lips, tongue and nostrils, razor blades in her ears, hair orange, pink and green and the caption said, 'I survived a Jewish mother!'

I felt suffocated by my mother's beliefs and the conditioning that she tried to impose on me out of her own fear and ignorance. But at the same time I clung to her because I was brainwashed to believe that I couldn't survive without her. It took therapy and 30 odd years of Yoga, fasts and brown rice diets to change the chemistry of this attachment.

But the most fundamental change was connecting to my innermost being that is beyond differences, my own connection to the life source without intermediaries.

Spiritual doesn't have to be dead – serious

Our ability to laugh at ourselves is a powerful tool for cutting through our tendency to take ourselves too seriously. Clowns and jesters have always been part of tribal life in aboriginal societies. Instead of going to therapists people in conflict would go to a jester who, by reflecting back the troubled one's attitudes, would help them see the funny side of their pomposity and arrogance enabling them to let go, to resolve the conflict and connect again to the community.

To me being spiritual means becoming aware that I am part of a larger reality and that the universe doesn't revolve around me. It means joining my will with God's will, listening for guidance, for being moved to speak or do. It means being aware of my own impermanence and meditating on it, which helps me to feel compassion for suffering… my own and others'.

True empathy is a spiritual quality. Periods of retreat and meditation in solitude are important in order to become more deeply grounded in the practice but it is the way we relate to other human beings and all of life every day that is the real arena. You'll be disappointed if you expect your third eye to open by closing the other two. 'Salvation' means 'safe return'. Return to your heart.

'Thy will be done' is the most difficult to practice. Somehow we feel that if we relinquish control, something terrible will happen. I suppose we'll no longer be able to deny death and that's what we're afraid of. It's easy to be a 'spiritual' person on holiday in a beautiful environment, feeling good and looking good with everything coming your way. But it's also possible that *when everything is coming your way you might be in the wrong lane!* Like this guy, driving on the motorway, and his mother phones and says, 'Darling, watch out! I just heard on the news that some maniac is driving down the motorway the wrong way. The son replies, 'And he's not the only one.'

It's when the disappointments come that it's much more difficult to accept them as part of God's will and to learn, from going deeply into the core of our discontent, to renew our purpose and say, 'Thy will be done.'

Love thy neighbor as thyself

'Open your mouth only if what you are going to say is more beautiful than silence'

Arab proverb

What really makes a difference to me is whether you listen to me with an open heart, acknowledging that fundamentally we are in the same boat; that we feel empathy for each other and that we can meet in our aloneness and companionship. Then we might find joy in our hearts. We are companions on the way, spiritual friends who are not trying to outsmart one another by our wit, intellect, and 'power clothes' or prove, 'I am right and you are wrong'.

If we can admit our vulnerability we can have a good laugh at our predicament, how precarious our existence and what a joke that we are trying to hide it from ourselves and each other, rather than getting on with whatever it is we are doing, simply, from the heart encouraging each other. Our wits become sharper, inspiring us to celebrate and have a song and a dance.

This is what I understand by 'love thy neighbor as thyself'... to wish other people what you wish for yourself... the gift of effortless being, in harmony with the laws of life, and with love in our hearts.

Shoulders are for shrugging

There is a common misconception that shoulders are for carrying burdens and heavy responsibility. That is the case if you are not in touch with your centre of gravity, the source of authentic power. Shoulders are for shrugging. They should be free and loose if you live and move from your centre. Let your shoulders drop onto your shoulder girdle. Let them come home.

The puzzled neck

The neck is a busybody; it will get involved in every movement if you let it. If you pay attention you'll notice that your neck is busy all the time. The way to release your neck is to connect to the root of your spine and experience the neck as continuation of the spine like a flower on top of the stem.

If the head is off centre the weight on the neck will be heavy. Rock your head like a delicately balanced weight and feel it becoming lighter. Then the neck will find its true alignment and support from the base.

The neck is puzzled because it doesn't know where it's meant to turn from. In fact the turning comes from the dorsal spine where the bra strap is; we all know where that is, women from experience and men from exploration. Most of us turn from the neck. For example, reversing in a car, the tendency is to move from the neck which creates a traffic jam in the spine and a lot of tension. The spine is meant to turn from the dorsal vertebrae. If you're turning to the right the left shoulder begins to move forward, the neck is uninvolved at this point. Once you've got the twist in the dorsal spine and the right shoulder has moved back and the left shoulder forward there is space in the neck to allow the head to turn and look over the right shoulder.

Perky Navel

Whether you are sitting, standing or walking, become aware of your navel; how it tends to collapse in a despondent sort of way! Become aware of your pubic bone in the centre and feel as if your navel is gradually growing from the pubic bone. That secure support at the base creates the upward releasing movement of the spine consequently opening the narrowest top chest cavity.

Yoga is not about *getting there;* it's about *being here*

*Let yourself be silently drawn by the strange pull of what
you really love. It will not lead you astray*

Jalaluddin Rumi

I remember how once, when I experienced a moment of what felt like 'presence', I wanted to hold on to it and be in the same state of mind later on, when I met up with a friend. Then I had another insight; *'You don't need to hold on; if you can be here now, you'll be able to be there then.'* For one moment I saw clearly that the place from which I experience presence is always here, it is a matter of connecting up to it. 'It' is the 'source', like the electricity current.

Forgiveness

'Oh, that's something I only know how to spell. I am not there yet, maybe when the sun begins to shine, and the weather gets warmer,' said J. when I mentioned forgiveness.

Forgiveness rises out of your heart as a consequence of having gone to the rock bottom of the pain of alienation that non-forgiveness creates, not because you are in a good mood and the sun is shining. It's easy to forgive when you are feeling good, but the resentment will come back when the inner clouds obscure the sun again.

Forgiveness is realizing that we are all in the same boat. It is wishing for oneself, as well as for everyone else, that we may be able to redeem our past mistakes and ignorance.

Making mistakes is part of our learning. Not being able to forgive yourself is a device to stay in the same old clutches. Being able to forgive yourself means facing the truth about yourself and moving on. We need to forgive ourselves and even those who don't forgive us.

> *'Let the wise guard their wandering thoughts*
> *Extremely subtle and difficult to perceive*
> *The thought that is well guarded*
> *Is the bearer of happiness'*

The Buddha

Practice of Yoga changes our relationship to pain — it becomes something to go through rather than something to avoid

I've noticed that being able to stand on my head for half an hour, or do a 'sensational' back-bend, making some people gasp with admiration, (which is what I was doing it for!), didn't increase the love in my heart. In fact, in the beginning it increased arrogance and pride.

So what did start awakening love in my heart?

Oh, living and suffering and gradually realizing that being constantly preoccupied with myself leads to isolation and loneliness.

Becoming aware of self- deception and developing a taste for being honest with myself.

'The Cloud of Unknowing' advises us to *'think of a Cloud of Forgetting between you and your sin* (sin in this sense of *missing the mark), and a Cloud of Unknowing between you and God'.* It feels reassuring that God and love cannot be defined or known by thinking.

You can only know what love is not. It is not judging, it is not holding grudges, it is not being competitive. It is not in one-upmanship, it is not in boasting. It is not in putting on airs; it is not in trying to impress. It is not in being arrogant; it is not in being divided.

Sometimes we want to give up in despair because it seems impossible to let go. And then something shifts and lets in a chink of light and it all seems all right again. Or, as Christopher Robin said about Winnie-the-Pooh, 'Silly old bear,' and everyone felt hopeful again.

The Things You Can Always Afford

To smile
To listen with heart
To be kind
Eat consciously
Not to speak harshly
Have a swing in your step
A song in your heart
And a twinkle in your eye

Right Effort

Upright not uptight
Relaxed not collapsed

Right effort is one of the fruits of continuous practice of Yoga with mindfulness. It is a way of practicing Yoga postures without straining.

In right effort there is no stress.

Becoming aware of the two-way movement of the spine, feeling the spine releasing upwards from the roots, finding the stillness and keeping this awareness in every position is the best antidote to stress I know of.

It means letting go of everything that blocks the grounding and lengthening of the spine and the flow of the breath.

Wrong effort is straining, trying too hard, trying to impress, trying to be 'the best', disconnecting from breathing, using will power to 'achieve' a posture rather than allowing it to unfold from the roots like a flower.

When we surrender all our tensions and grasping and connect to the vital energy in stillness, each posture becomes a prayer.

'How to get your knickers in a healthy twist', said my friend Nina in jest!

I'm never bored...

… because there's always an inner and outer show going on if I am into watching my thoughts and my feelings and not just blindly reacting to what's going on. I can breathe and relax and not get into a knot about things I don't like or get overly elated about things I do like, in other words attempt equilibrium; practice concentration. It doesn't mean there aren't times when I want to get the hell out of a situation and observe my thoughts and feelings later.

I am not responsible for the thoughts that arise in my mind but I am responsible for how I respond to them. Don't try to stop negative thoughts, just don't entertain them.

The Head

A Chi Gung centering exercise:
Feet on earth
Head to the sky
Body relaxes
Mind expands
Be quiet and respectful
Entire body in harmony with Chi

The head should be up there in a dignified fashion, balanced on top of the atlas. When the neck is stiff it is a sign that we are pulled up into the head, too much thinking and not enough awareness. If the head is centred and balanced there will be no strain on the neck. In order for that to happen the body must be grounded at the base of the spine.

To free the neck and allow the head to balance we need to let go of the attitudes we've accumulated in the upper body and surrender to the ground. A head that is held habitually to one side, or thrown back, makes the neck muscles tense. Allowing the spine to find its axis from the root will bring the neck into its natural alignment. The head balances easily on its support when the main structure of the whole body is in balance.

Become aware of the freedom in your neck.
Imagine your neck starting from the root of your spine.
Free the base of your scull.
Let your head gently release upwards and balance effortlessly on top of the Atlas.

This will align your head with the axis of your spine.

If all of us humans on this planet would stand from the feet upward, and think of the head as the last to come in line with the spine, like a flower on top of the stem, the world would become a friendlier place!

Have mercy on the base of your skull!

This is where the spinal chord and the brain meet, so it makes sense to keep it free and flowing.

Make tiny little nodding movements like a Mandarin doll, backwards and forwards and side to side, the smaller the movement the deeper the feeling connection.
Become aware of the freedom in your neck.
Imagine your neck starting from the root of your spine.
Free the base of your scull.
Let your head gently release upwards and balance effortlessly on top of the Atlas.
This will align your head with the axis of your spine.

The base of the skull, where a lot of tension accumulates and where obstinacy sits, is where the spinal cord reaches the brain. Let go of the tension, and allow freedom of circulation, so that the natural cranial rhythm is restored. Make tiny little nodding movements like a Mandarin doll, backwards and forwards and side to side, the smaller the movement the deeper the feeling connection.

My first "Aha" experience

I said to my psychotherapist R.D. Laing, 'my life feels like a nightmare.' He replied, 'it's easier to wake up from a nightmare than a pleasant dream.' 'Aha,' I thought, 'in this scheme of things I seem to have an advantage; if I'm in a nightmare, there is more incentive to wake up!'

Take care

What are we talking about when we say 'Take care'?
Take care not to fall under a passing car as you go out into the street.
Take care to eat a good and balanced diet.
Take care not to eat too much or too little.
Take care not to sleep too much or too little.
Take care that you are not too hot or too cold.
Take care to take enough exercise.

But what about …?

Take care to let your breath move freely.
Take care to let your shoulders drop away from your ears and
onto your shoulder girdle.
Take care to let your spine be free and release upwards from its root.
Take care to feel the contact of your feet with the ground.
Take care to let your head balance.
Take care to have pleasure in movement letting your movements flow.
Take care to be more peaceful.
Take care to touch the inner stillness.
Take care to speak with kindness.
Take care not to be a danger to yourself.

Take care to be present.

There's always time

Make an appointment with yourself first thing in the morning. Get out of bed and onto the floor to give yourself some time to unwind and centre yourself. Lie on the floor for a few minutes, letting your spine release and align.

Become quiet and aware of your breathing. Let it flow. You might become aware that your breathing is blocked and un-rhythmical. How do you let your breath flow?

Start from what you are aware of at this moment. Acknowledge what is on your mind; give yourself a lot of space with all your thoughts and feelings. If you are feeling sad, feel the sadness. You might feel sad but your heart and mind are connected.

'I have no time,' many people complain.

There is always time. Be honest, you are looking for excuses.

When you are busy doing chores and the kids want your attention, and you feel distraught that you don't have the time to practise Yoga, think for a moment that you can bring mindfulness into whatever you are doing. You don't need any special time for it. How empowering is this thought!

Allowing just ten minutes in the morning to lie down on the floor consciously, to align your body, to take a few breaths, to make contact with gravity, to let there be space in your chest for your lungs and heart to function freely. To harmonise your breathing and to give your inner world some attention is at least as much a part of hygiene as spending hours deodorising yourself at the edges.

Stiffening up in the night

T. says, 'I feel more freedom in my hip joints. I feel more grounded in the root of my spine and my neck feels released. I am really happy about it.… aagh!.. but I'm going to stiffen up in the night and wake up stiff again.'

'It often happens that you experience relief from tension and then the tension springs back again. The force of old habits is very strong. That's why repeated practise is needed to get to the bottom of what's behind the habits and to make the relaxed state more enduring and conscious.'

'But why should I get stiff during my sleep?'

'In sleep, when the cat's away the mice can play, the ego with its controlling power is asleep, so the emotional patterns from the unconscious emerge, affecting the body and the breathing patterns. If your emotional patterns are not resolved the body reacts by tensing up. That's why you wake up tense. In the morning it is essential to clear the effect of the night. Lie on the floor and relax. Wait for your breath to release and become more rhythmical, more harmonious.'

'Yes, they don't spend enough money on research about sleep. They don't understand sleep.'

'Whether *they* understand sleep or not, it's not necessarily going to help you understand why *you* wake up stiff after a night's sleep. The important thing is to keep getting in touch with your tensions and deeper emotional structures and release them consciously, then you'll be able to have a relaxed night's sleep and wake up refreshed.'

'My doctor says I'm depressed'

I think a state of emergency should be declared when people don't know what they feel and wait for the doctor to tell them!

Anxiety and depression are veils we put over our feelings. If we learn to get in touch with our feelings, recognise, acknowledge and stay with them we might be less likely to succumb to depression, or, if we are depressed, recognise that we are depressed and look at what lies behind the depression.

A. says, 'I am so relieved. The doctor said it's a virus. I couldn't understand why I've been feeling tired and run down for so long. It's such a relief!'

Yes, it is a virus, but it still doesn't absolve you of the need to be present to what was going on before you 'caught' the virus and after. Attending to and being honest about what is happening in your mind and body, and relaxing with it will prevent stagnant energy accumulating in the body where viruses have a chance to breed. Keeping the energy flowing strengthens your immune system.

First of all, let's be honest. It is self-deception that is responsible for most disease. How do *we* contribute to our unease? This is not blame! We have to touch our pain fully, make friends with it, accept it, without editing it, then it has its own way of transformation. Books and wisdom don't help unless we apply what is being taught and make it our own experience.

Mina Semyon

Awareness in everyday life

'Dear ones, let's anoint this earth with dance!'

Hafiz

In the kitchen

Become aware of how you stand in the kitchen while cooking or washing the dishes. You can save a lot of energy by simply being aware of your feet on the ground, dropping your shoulders and. breathing. Breathe while washing the dishes; breathe while cooking. Sometimes tenderness awakens and your heart opens just by taking care to wash a cup 'behind the ears'.

Waiting for the bus

Become aware of your feet and how they touch the ground. Don't worry; nobody can see you doing it. Let your weight go down into your feet, allowing your neck to relax. Let go of your head. Let your breath relax. At the same time acknowledge the surroundings. It won't make the bus come quicker but it will save you getting a headache and becoming irritable.

'Yes, yes,' you might say, 'It's all very well to be so smart if you don't have to stand in the freezing cold when you're late for work and the bus doesn't come.'

Life has a way of challenging our theories by presenting us with the opportunity to test them. I wrote the above before my car got stolen. After it was stolen I was given the opportunity to test my ability to relax while waiting for a bus on a drizzly Thursday morning and being late for a class.

I found myself thinking, 'OK, you've been talking about it, now show your mettle.'

And it wasn't easy. Some devil inside obstinately made me want to be restless and tense and irritable rather than do what I know is sensible.

So I said to myself, 'If you can't be sensible and reasonable and do what you know is best, then be irritable, restless and tense. On the other hand if you can be sensible, relax, breathe and watch your emotions, then do that. The bus will come when it comes.'

Sometimes the best we can do is to be aware of how resistant we are to practising what we are preaching.

As a wise master said, 'The one who knows but doesn't act accordingly, knows imperfectly.'

Sitting in a car, stuck in traffic

Stuck in your car in endless traffic?

Think, 'There is nothing at all I can do about it. If I give in to getting agitated, angry and frustrated I'll get more tired, get a headache, raise my blood pressure and most probably have an argument when I get home.'

For those who are capable of being reasonable for their own good, this is an intelligent thing to do. But how often do we know but go against what we know? When we will ever learn is hard to say, but hopefully when we observe the consequences of our own actions and look at them honestly, we'll learn from experience.

So… if you can… slow down, breathe out, make the exhalation longer. Feel your sitting bones in touch with the seat, release the spine between the shoulder blades, release your neck and exhale with a long hissing sound to help you exhale fully.

Make a sound, 'Ahhhhhh', like Marilyn Monroe in 'Ahhhhhh Wanna Be Loved by You'.

You might feel less inclined to hoot and shout at the person in front of you who is in the same situation, poor devil, and you might come home in a surprisingly good mood. It's not the situation itself that makes us irritable; it's our attitude to it.

Sitting in the dentist's chair

Your head thrown back, your mouth wide open, the dentist's fingers in your mouth and the sound of the drill in your ears. Your neck is tensed, your shoulders hunched, and your breathing almost stops.

Not the most pleasant situation in the world, but why add more tension to it? See if you can possibly find it in yourself, even under these conditions, to try and claim your inner space. You might as well become aware of your contact with the seat, sink into it, become aware of your breath, which is tight in anticipation, and exhale quietly without being too demonstrative.

Acknowledge your fear. Say to yourself, *'This is fear'*, and breathe out a long breath. Then breathe in from the lower abdomen and breathe out again.

It will relax the dentist, so he or she will do a better job, and you will avoid getting too much pressure in the head and neck, and remain centred as far as possible, under the circumstances.

A relaxed dentist

A dentist in my class said, 'It's all very well talking about being at ease and letting go, but I can't do it when I am leaning over patients all day long.'

'But wouldn't it be wonderful to have a relaxed dentist?'

Someone else said, 'I once had a relaxed dentist and he was useless.'

Of course you don't want a surgeon who is cool and laid back at the expense of his skills. It's a fine balance between being relaxed and acutely present at the same time.

In the beginning most people fall asleep during relaxation after a Yoga class because it's very hard to maintain this fine level of being relaxed and alert at the same time. Most people associate alertness with being stressed and relaxation with falling asleep.

High-powered means that you are expected to be wired. In fact you are most alive and vital when you can let go and relax allowing all the functions in the body to do their job effortlessly. When we get out of the way then vitality is there at its highest.

At work

If people would only take the space to lie down on the floor consciously a couple of times a day for five minutes, to release the spine and let it find it's balance in relation to gravity, there would be less stress and lower back pain in the world! If there is no space to lie down then:

Stand next to your desk, put your hands on the desk with your feet apart the width of your hips and your heels slightly wider than your toes. Lean into your wrists, let your head hang; take a couple of long breaths. Then walk back till your spine is straight, feel your hips stretching away from your wrists, like two ends of a piece of elastic stretching away from each other. Keep your feet in line with the hips. Breathe out to the base of the spine, letting the shoulders relax.

In the shower

I asked a new student, 'How are you getting on?'

She said, 'I don't practise the postures yet, but I do pay attention to how I stand in the shower and I feel better straight away and also afterwards.'

After the gym

A student asked, 'What should I practice after a work-out in the gym?'

'Lie down on the floor with your knees to your chest, give yourself a hug, cross your feet the opposite way to your arms and breathe gently. Then cross your feet and arms the other way and again let go and breathe. This will allow your spine to release to its natural alignment, and release any tensions accumulated in the workout'.

At the airport

The plane is delayed, the departure lounge is chock-a-block with people and luggage, you are hot and restless, and your eyes are taking in too much movement and your ears too much noise.

The good news is that the outside commotion doesn't have to invade your whole being. Inner silence does not depend on the absence of noise.

Stop, just where you are, don't change anything, become aware of your feet touching the ground.

Become aware of your breathing.

Exhale deeply, feel your feet becoming more grounded, and your upper body releasing in response, like a tree.

Say to yourself, 'Calming my whole body I breathe in, calming my mind I breathe out.'

Jet lag

There is a story about a Red Indian chief who was being driven in a car at fast speed to a conference. After an hour he asked the driver to stop, got out, sat at the curb by the side of the road and just kept on sitting.

The driver asked, 'What's up?'

The Chief replied, 'I am waiting for my soul to catch up.'

Many people doubt that there is such a thing as a soul, but most people experience jet lag. Imagine the distances we cover while flying in a plane at tremendous speed of which we are not conscious except in theory. We've spent some time in a foreign place, met people and have a sense of that place in our body and mind.

By keeping conscious of all the stages of the journey and staying in touch with your breathing, you'll find the effects of jet lag will be milder, the coming down to earth smoother and the adjustment to the time difference easier. You'll find that you are together body and soul when you arrive.

Passing a driving test

I learnt through experience that if I kept on studying and revising more and more in a nervous sort of state I'd be hopeless at passing my driving test. But if I created harmonious conditions in my body by staying mindful of my thoughts, practising letting them go and staying with my breathing rhythm, I'd become more balanced and relaxed. Then what I'd learned would be more accessible to me when I needed it. Before the test I practised Yoga, trusting that I'd learned enough and that it wouldn't run away if I relaxed. That's how I passed my driving test after failing it twice.

You don't have to disconnect at the party!

I think there is a popular misconception that being spiritual doesn't go with being glamorous and having fun. Glamorous doesn't have to be empty and superficial. Fun doesn't have to be flippant. You don't have to put on airs and disconnect from your centre because you are wearing fishnet stockings with red garters and a feather boa if that happens to be your whim at the moment.

The social pressure to be interesting

There is only one thing I find boring and that is the social pressure to be 'interesting'. There was a time when I used to have a notebook with jokes in it and before going to a party I'd memorise a few so that I'd have at least something to say.

It's fear of silence that makes your mind race, forcing you to think of something to say. And before you know it there is solid tension between you and the other person, emanating from your tense bodies. If we can just be together, giving each other and ourselves breathing space to be quiet and silent until we are moved by the spirit to say something - or not… what a relief! Then there is a chance for something authentic to happen between us, even if it's *'only'* silence.

Try this exercise:

If in a social situation a thought comes up, 'I am not interesting, I have nothing to say,' say to yourself, 'I have nothing to say at this moment, I accept it, I breathe and relax. I just am, neither interesting nor uninteresting. I feel whole.'

If we could become comfortable with ourselves we wouldn't be afraid of silence and if we weren't afraid of silence we would feel comfortable.

Synchronicity Miracle

A young friend Amy sent a text message at 7am asking for a little advice. We had a few back and forth text exchanges. A while later she asked: 'Can you talk briefly?' I replied:' I am now walking to Primrose Hill but I can walk and talk'. She phoned and we talked, talked about dealing with challenging times, about taking responsibility for one's own feelings, about caring, listening etc... We were quite deep in conversation when suddenly I stopped in mid- sentence as I saw her standing outside her car on the side of the road (we live a fair distance from each other). It was very funny because for a moment I felt annoyed at being interrupted, like 'what are you doing interrupting me when I am talking to you?' It was a miraculous moment that dispelled all the issues and created a lot of fun and laughter. We ended up having coffee and a poached egg on toast each, in the nearby cafe, before going off to work in much lighter spirits!

A day in my life

Had a lovely lunch, strange combination, courgette cakes and Pizza Pecorino, but utterly delicious, shared with a friend, and then a walk across Hampstead Heath, both of us singing a Russian-Yiddishe song 'Tumbalalaika', which ends with 'Let Joy Be'!. Had to get back to my studio and a Yoga session, which turned into helping someone let go of being in the grip of anger by breathing, slowing down, doing a few stretches, finally leading to turning their thinking around. Felt a flow of transforming energy with gratitude. Who could ask for anything more!

Finding your feet

Forget everything you've ever been told about what it means to 'stand on your own two feet' and find your own connection to Mother Earth and the sky above. It is high up on the evolutionary scale to have our feet firmly on the ground and to let our bodies release upwards.

Human beings stood up on two feet. The debate is still going on about what this means. Having our feet on the ground certainly doesn't mean being mundane and boring and forgetting our dreams. Anyone with even a drop of Gypsy in their soul will know that giving up on our dreams just won't do.

'They' told us, *Stand on your own two feet,* but omitted to tell us that if we did we'd experience tremendous freedom in our whole being, we wouldn't be all top-heavy with no foundation.

Standing can become relaxing and interesting

We'd never be bored, and our muscle tone would remain alive and 'interested', even in a simple standing position, if we'd stay in touch with the vitality needed for the constant rediscovery of our balance. Rediscovering and securing a well-integrated position while standing frees the muscles of their old habits.

A baby learning to stand enjoys an exciting game of losing and finding his/her balance. We need to carry on this exciting game for the rest of our lives.

An avid student of Buddhism would often discuss the teachings with a Master who lived across the river. One day the student felt inspired and wrote the following poem:

> *I bow my head to the heaven within heaven*
> *Hairline rays illuminating the universe*
> *The eight winds cannot move me*
> *Sitting still upon the purple golden lotus*

Impressed by himself, the student dispatched somebody to deliver this poem to the Master. He felt certain that the Master would be just as impressed, maybe even recognize his enlightenment.

The "eight winds" in the poem referred to praise, ridicule, honour, disgrace, gain, loss, pleasure and misery - interpersonal forces of the material world that drive and influence the hearts of men. The student was saying that he had attained a higher level of spirituality, where these forces no longer affected him.

Smiling, the Master wrote, *"FART"* on the manuscript and had it returned to the student across the river.

Expecting compliments and a seal of approval, the student was shocked when he saw what the Master had written.

He hit the roof, *"How dare he insult me like this? Why that lousy old Master! He's got a lot of explaining to do!"*

Full of indignation, the student got into a boat and ferried himself to the other shore as quickly as possible. Once there, he jumped off and charged into the hut where the Master lived. He wanted to find the Master and demand an apology.

He found the Master's door closed. On the door was a piece of paper, with the following two lines:

> *'The eight winds cannot move me,*
> *One fart blows me across the river'.*

How I spent the night with jealousy

H. didn't ring and didn't come that evening. I couldn't make contact with him either. He had spent every night with me for a year or so. My mind was in a spin: 'He is with another woman.'

I was supposed to be giving a workshop on Yoga and Mindfulness the following morning with L. In the grip of jealousy I felt what a fraud I was going to feel the next day, talking about mindfulness and observing our thoughts and emotions, letting them go and bringing attention to our breathing. And besides I'd be tired as I was unable to sleep. I told myself that the workshop would be a failure. I tossed and turned and made cups of tea waiting for the phone to ring. I tried to practice mindfulness; 'Ok, acknowledge your thoughts, *he is with another woman*, and breeeeeathe in, *he is with another woman* and breeeeeathe out,' but the grip of jealousy in my solar plexus wouldn't go away. I prayed, 'Please, don't let me be a fraud.'

Then I thought, 'OK, I want to be with him but my companion for the night is jealousy. Hello jealousy, we are going to spend the night together. I feel jealous and I breathe in, I feel jealous and I breathe out.' I surrendered to jealousy and finally fell asleep. In the morning I woke up still feeling jealous but I didn't feel a fraud. I thought, 'I'm not claiming perfection, I'm practising mindfulness to the degree of which I am capable at this moment. I feel jealousy but I am not beside myself with jealousy.' Intimacy with jealousy helped me to maintain presence.

'Here let me help you', said the monkey, putting the fish up the tree'

To be of help to others we need to watch out not to put our hidden agendas onto other people in the name of helping. Ronnie Laing used to quote the Hippocratic Oath, 'Do no harm', emphasizing that one can do harm by 'trying' to 'do good'; he also said, 'One human cannot wake another up; the best we can do is not to sing lullabies to those who are waking up.'

My understanding of 'not trespassing' is having respect for the other's inner sanctum, the inviolate place within.

My aim in my classes is to create space for each of us to experience our presence together, giving us glimpses of faith, based on our own experience, that there is life beyond our habitual preoccupations. Presence is nearer to us than our breath.

Each individual unfolds and grows according to his or her own pace and rhythm, and the important thing in helping is not to get in the way of that unfolding. A good teacher will give instructions and encourage the confidence that is already within the student. I think that the only authentic help we can give is that of helping others to help themselves to get in touch with what's already there.

What do I teach and what lies behind the persona of a Yoga teacher?

I ask myself this question regularly so that I don't get stuck in any specific attitude. I don't want to have to pretend that I am beyond anger, fear, jealousy, envy, craving praise, fearing blame. It's too tiring to have to pretend. I practice relaxing with whatever I am feeling, letting go and at the same time, connecting to my centre, breathing and aligning my body in relation to gravity, as the good Lord intended.

If I honestly acknowledge and accept what is on my mind at the beginning of the class and don't try to change or manipulate it, relaxing and tuning in to my breathing rhythm, I notice that my heart opens and I am there for others in a genuine way. And that is what I like to share with others; becoming conscious of the body's alignment, of breathing, of how thoughts and emotions affect the flow of energy and how intimately inter-connected they are.

The first thing I am concerned with when I am working with others is to relax myself and not strain to help. How can I help another relax if I get all tensed up myself? Most of all I like doing nothing, in the spirit of Taoist wu wei, effortless effort, letting the creative energy flow through me whether I am working, reading, writing or helping someone else. I never make a plan but practice tuning myself up and if I am in tune the lesson flows. I notice how I tense up if I try to put a point across, if I am trying to change people.

I go through periods of asking myself, 'What am I doing teaching other people; is it a case of the blind leading the blind?' It is useful not to be afraid to ask this question. It deepens our connection to the source, taking us to the very root of our experience. I endeavor to stay at the source of creative energy and let it guide me; let it whisper in my ear.

Before each session I pray, 'If two or more are gathered together in the name of the truth, the way and the light, there the holy spirit shall be in their midst. May I be a channel for the healing of all the people present in this room and those who are absent'. And at the end of the session I say thanks and pray, 'May this session be of benefit to everyone present and absent and may I not take credit for the healing that sometimes happens.'

My classes are not about becoming stretch addicts. A good stretch is very pleasant and beneficial but the next minute you could be disconnected again! My classes are about awakening our awareness of the interconnectedness of our whole being. To be whole – healthy – to realize our 'being' requires nothing less than total surrender. This is the cream, the 'royal jelly' of the practice, if we dare to open our hearts and listen to our inner voice.

Mina Semyon

Start by doing nothing

*The entry into your being is through
what is happening at this moment in your mind and body*

Stop and become quiet. Listen. Most of us have a lot of noise going on in our heads, which we wish we could stop. 'Why did I say that? I wish I hadn't. Why didn't she call me? She never calls me; I always have to call her. The world is a mess, so what's the point? Life is unfair. I wish I could live by the sea…' and before you know it you're in a spin.

Your muscles respond to all your thoughts and emotions if you are not conscious of the process. Your shoulders go up to your ears, your chest becomes tight, you clench your jaw, your neck becomes rigid and pretty soon you're exhausted and don't know why. All that wasted energy!

I once spent a whole year being jealous of a non-existent female harp-player!

My partner, a musician and composer, told me in a moment of inspiration, that he had decided to put a harp into his composition. Instantly, like lightening, I was inflamed by jealousy. I saw this harp player, a beautiful young woman with her exquisite fingers plucking the strings of the harp. I'd wake up at night racking my brain whether I'd ever seen a male harp player. No! They are always women! In the end he took the harp out…

Sometimes the noise in the head reaches unbearable proportions. You can't stop it by using willpower. The release comes by making friends with your thoughts, relaxing with them. I find this mindfulness exercise helpful:

*Aware of the activities in my mind I breathe in.
Aware of the activities in my mind I breathe out.*

After a while of acknowledging the mind's activities they begin to calm down and you become aware that there *is* stillness at the centre of the storm.

How can death be bad for you?

Paradise —
I see flowers
from the cottage where I lie.

Yaitsu's death poem, 1807

In my childhood in a suburb of Moscow death was a nasty subject, to be hidden, not to be spoken about, to be avoided at all costs, creating tension, unease, dis-ease, so we were already more dead than alive.

When my mother heard someone had died she used to spit three times over her shoulder, *'tsfu, tsfu. tsfu'* and say, *'It shouldn't happen to us'*.

Occasionally when a Communist Party member died they carried him in an open coffin through the streets of our suburb Khimki, accompanied by brass wind instruments playing window- rattling funeral marches.

My mother would rush to close the windows trying to protect me from the extreme gloom that every reminder of death had provoked since my father died when I was four.

We human beings think we are different from everything else on earth. But everything is born and dies and we sort of know it applies to us as well, but 'we with our superior intelligence must be able to find a way out of this predicament'. We just can't come to terms with it and live and let live while we are still alive. When I first heard about the Buddhist contemplation on death I couldn't even imagine getting started.

Learning how to let go continuously can allow us to go through the stages of life as a natural process, including ageing and dying. Dying could then perhaps be akin to a leaf falling from a tree. Yes, it is sad to realise the impermanence of everything and everybody near and dear including ourselves. So we can begin by relaxing with the sadness, which will open and mellow our hearts.

'Oy, am I stiff,' people say, but who says,
'Oy, my heart is closed; I can't feel sadness, tenderness, love, sorrow.'

If you can relax with your feelings,
You can be sad and relaxed.
You can be sad and not depressed.
You can feel fear and not be afraid of feeling it.

There is a private joke between airline staff when they talk about safety on board and suggest that in case of emergency you put your head between your knees. 'Put your head between your knees,' they say over the loudspeaker, and then, to each other '… and kiss your arse goodbye!' So maybe this is one of the advantages of becoming supple through the practice of Yoga.

> *'I died as a mineral and became a vegetable.*
> *I passed away as vegetation and became animal.*
> *Leaving the animal state I became Man.*
> *Why should I fear?*
> *When was I less through death?*
> *I shall once more die from manhood to soar with angels,*
> *and I must go beyond angelhood - all perish but God.*
> *When I have given up my angel-self, I shall be what no mind has conceived'.*

Rumi

Husband and wife

I was teaching Yoga to a mother and a daughter in the master bedroom of a suburban mansion.

The husband comes in, watches the class for a few minutes and says to his wife, 'I'm glad that for a change you have to do what someone else is telling you to do.'

Self-fulfilling prophecy or 'you can keep your fucking jack' syndrome

Sometimes we can perceive the present in terms of our past experience of disappointment or being let down, which can create a self-fulfilling prophecy of more disappointment.

Like this guy who is driving down the deserted country road in the middle of the night and suddenly gets a flat tire. He gets out of the car, looks in the boot and discovers that he hasn't got a jack. What to do? He's cold and hungry and wants to get home. He remembers passing a farmhouse a few miles back. OK, there's nothing else to do but start walking back.

He walks and walks and while he walks, he starts imagining what might happen when he gets there. 'They might not be in… the farmer might not have a jack… or he'll be so angry at being woken up in the middle of the night that he'll slam the door in my face. He might even have a gun…'

As he gets nearer the house he gets more and more worked up, more and more certain the farmer will be furious, refuse to help him and tell him to beat it. As he gets closer to the door he mutters to himself, 'The guy is a selfish bastard…' He knocks on the door, muttering away, and when the farmer comes out in his pajamas the guy shouts in his face: 'You can keep your fucking jack'

Yoga and the Ageing Process

The older we get the more playful our joints!

'I'm not ageing – I'm ripening to perfection'

The good news is that our joints don't have to become rigid through ageing. Scientists have discovered that DNA has a capacity for self-repair and that it is also influenced by our every thought, feeling and action.

Yes! By paying attention to your mind, body and breath, and their interrelatedness, you can become lighter, freer and healthier, and your immune system, stronger. By tuning in to your inherent balance you can create ease and conditions for healing. Your joints can become playful with age!

Imagine! You step out of your own way and let your body do its magic! It will work effortlessly and harmoniously. If we could just drop all the resistance we'd feel free, but since we often can't, we have to keep getting in touch with the resistance and letting go of it gradually by degrees.

And if you can let go in one leap of faith, good for you!

Menopause

'Ten thousand flowers in spring
the moon in autumn
a cool breeze in summer
snow in winter
If your mind isn't clouded
by unnecessary things
this is the season
of your life'.

Wu-Men 1183-1260

Does this year's spring regret being so much older than the spring of many years ago? 'Oy, I was so much younger then.'

In autumn, does the birch tree knit its brow and get anxious when autumn leaves start to fall?

Growing old? The important word, surely, is *growing* and we never stop growing. Maybe we don't have to turn life into a series of crises if we stay present and go with the flow through all the different stages of life.

Women are forced into the collective image of what it means to be a post-menopausal woman. A woman of any age can be a going concern in all her compartments if she stays in tune with the life in her, as well as all the anxieties and despairs. As Mae West said, 'It's not the men in my life, it's the life in my men.' If you let your energy flow your honeyed secretions don't have to dry up because you are no longer nineteen.

Getting the grannies out of the groin

See if you can begin to enjoy being in the moment, being mindful, whether you're sitting, standing, lying down or walking. Then you might get the potential for hot flushes out of your groin even before the menopause. That's where they have been hiding in women for generations, in socially imposed limitations and inhibitions.

Get your grannies out of your groin. It's never too late and never too early. We are all flowers in different stages of unfolding.

Menopause is not a disease unless you make it into one by resisting the natural process. Let the energy flow, menopause or no menopause. Menopause doesn't have to be meno-poisonous.

Free your groin, inhabited by the ghosts of many generations not allowed to feel their bodies, not allowed to swing their hips. Get your grannies out of all your nooks and crannies! Evict them! Let them join in the great cosmic dance. That's what we can do for our ancestors – release them.

When I say this in a class most people laugh spontaneously, but occasionally someone asks, 'what kind of Yoga is that?' What I mean by 'grannies in your groin' is all the conditioning that got lodged in there over generations, the groin being a particular place for storing sexual inhibition.

Each generation has the responsibility to liberate itself a little more from traditional fixed ideas. Tradition!

'But what about honouring my ancestors?'

'Maybe the best thing you can do to honour your ancestors is to let them out of your body and set them free.'

We would need a lot less medical interference and the National Health Service wouldn't be so overloaded if we could just become aware and let go of some of the inhibiting conditioning that is blocking our energy flow.

'How does becoming aware help?'

If you knew you were digging your nails into your palm wouldn't you be foolish to keep digging them deeper? If you are not aware of doing it you will go on even though it's obviously self-destructive. So who can argue with that?

And don't worry about what kind of Yoga this is. Call it 'Sensible Yoga', or 'Basmati Yoga'. Often what it is called becomes more important than the experience of it. First experience it and then see what you want to call it. This is what those Yogis did. They just practised and practised in the forests in India and then expressed what they experienced and passed it on to us, which is great. All the same we have to find our own experience of Yoga, otherwise we are hooked into dogma. It becomes a case of 'My *karma* has just run over your *dogma?*' Have a laugh. Your sense of humour is intimately connected with freedom in your body. Laugh from your belly! Doctors should check patients for dangerously low levels of sense of humour.

This guy falls off the cliff and just manages to hang on to a branch. So he's hanging up there and praying: 'Please help, anybody there?' A voice comes 'Yes, I am here, let go of the branch and my arms will be there to catch you.' The guy thinks for a moment and says: 'Anybody else up there?'

I am addicted to wholeness...

which means subtracting, rather than adding; letting go of straining that blocks the free flow of breath. In Yoga there is such a term as 'right effort' which means letting my will surrender to 'thy will'. It doesn't mean that it's easy, there are still times of conflict and struggle until recognition dawns that there is no need to hold on to anything, and there is nothing to hold on to.

Mula Nasrudin went out for a walk with a friend, it started to rain, Nasrudin opened his umbrella, but it was full of holes. The friend asked 'why did you bring an umbrella full of holes?' Nasrudin replied, 'because I didn't think it would rain.'

The body in religion

I find myself wondering about how the body has been excommunicated from religion because of its desires and appetites. But surely until we can take responsibility for our own choices, there will always be an outside authority that has the final say? In some religions a man is not supposed to look at a woman he is not married to, let alone touch her, not even shake hands. Surely if the body is busy keeping all desires under lock and key it's bound to be tense and uncomfortable. Is it not possible for a spiritual human being to act appropriately out of choice, moral, ethical, sensible choice, and not just rigidly obey rules?

Take as long as it takes

How long will it take to remember to remember?

R. sits on the floor with her legs stretched out in front trying to bend forward and touch her feet. She strains, she loses contact with the ground, pulls up into her shoulders and neck and alarmingly holds her breath.

I put my hands on her shoulders, massaging them gently, leaving my hands on her shoulders until her breathing relaxes and becomes deeper. 'Breathe down into the hips and let your spine lengthen up to the sky.

After the class she thanks me, 'I've really learned something important about grounding and releasing. The problem is how to remember?'

With practice remembering to slow down and feel your body grounded in the base and releasing upwards like a tree becomes a good habit.

I used to write at the end of my shopping list:

Milk
Butter
Vegetables
Fruit
Flowers
Don't forget to thank God

I thought that if I practiced gratitude, even if I didn't feel it, it might become real in the end. If you can't make it, fake it. Eventually gratitude started to replace discontent.

How long will it take before we stop looking for love everywhere other than in our own hearts?

Like Mula Nasrudin looking for his keys under a lamp post.

Someone asked, 'Is this where you lost them?'

'No', replied Nasrudin, 'but it's lighter here.'

'God send me patience but please hurry'

Imagine! There is a magnolia tree, symbol of inner and outer peace, the flower of patience, which blossoms only every sixteen years.

How long will it take to stop waiting for everything to be all right before we start breathing freely?

How long will it take to stop resenting the muddy patches we all sometimes need to go through?

Like the picture on a card someone sent me of God parting the Red Sea to let Moses and his people pass from Egypt to the land of milk and honey, from darkness into light, from bondage to freedom.

All the people are standing hesitantly on the shore and Moses is saying,

'What do you mean, it's a bit muddy?'

'Before we start 'the Yoga'…..'

S. talks about her relationship to her illness: 'I'm having orthodox medical intervention but I am also addressing it from a holistic point of view. Through my illness I am becoming more aware of how the illness has come to be, that it is a consequence of accumulated denial of pain and hurt in childhood which I've never addressed in an embodied way.'

'I am having acupuncture treatments and homeopathy. I find it hard sometimes to withstand the conventional doctor's diagnosis and prognosis. I need to find courage, without being reckless, to stand my ground. I am actually getting better and feel that in the long run it will be Yoga and increasing awareness that will heal me.'

While she talks I sit on the floor cross-legged, keeping up awareness of my contact with the ground and breathing which doesn't diminish the quality of my listening and being present, on the contrary it makes it sharper. She is also sitting on the floor but I can see from the way she is sitting that she is not applying what she knows to the sitting posture while she is talking. Somehow the sitting and the talking seem separate.

Then she says, 'One more thing before we start the Yoga.'

I say, 'There is no separation between 'the Yoga' and what we are talking about now. While you are talking you can still be aware of your breathing and contact with the ground. You said earlier that you've been feeling good but it doesn't last. Suddenly for no good reason you are feeling bad again. I believe that connecting your awareness with ordinary activities, by letting this connection grow and become stronger your sense of well being will become more consistent.'

Gratitude to teachers past and present

Namaste

What are we doing when we press our palms together and bow to each other in the Indian tradition?

> *I honor the place in you where the entire universe resides;*
> *I honor the place in you that is of love, of truth, of light, of peace.*
> *When you are in that place in you*
> *And I am in that place in me,*
> *We are truly present to each other.*

I would like to acknowledge the loving guidance of all my teachers in this difficult, ongoing process of awakening to authentic being.

Gratitude is a feeling that arises out of the depths of one's being. When it happens a glimpse of light appears, and we feel connected to all of life and feel part of it instead of isolated in our ego shell, made up of all our familiar likes and dislikes, fears, worries and preoccupations.

It is not necessary to belong to a religious sect, or to follow a guru to be devoted to God. The deepest devotion is to remember respect for life in all its forms and to feel love in our hearts.

I discovered that my pain and suffering come from not being able to slow down enough to experience this respect and thankfulness.

The more I practice the more I realize how much fortitude is required to stay on this inner path towards liberation. Respect and gratitude awaken towards those people, past and present, who have been inspiring examples guiding me to recognize the different stages and not become discouraged by difficulties and obstacles on the way.

The fact that they *all* said that it is difficult is somehow encouraging, as is the fact that they all said *'don't look to me, look within'*. Most of all it is being present and mindful of what is happening in our inner and outer world that is the true teacher and healer.

Take it with two pinches of salt

We need to question all 'authority' and all traditions and not just follow them blindly. 'Respectful irreverence' is what I mean by 'take it with two pinches of salt' With all due respect to teachers and teachings… wake up, feel and think for yourself.

Listen to the silence in your heart
Find love within yourself
Make your body supple and coordinated
Keep your heart open.

There is life and light and joy and freshness yet.
May everyone enjoy good health and happiness.

Printed in the United States
By Bookmasters